Unshakeable
F.O.C.U.S

**FAITH TO OVERCOME
CIRCUMSTANCES USING POSITIVE
SUGGESTIONS**

JERMAIN MILLER

Copyright © 2020 by Jermain Miller

All rights reserved. No part of this publication may be reproduced, distributed or transmitted in any form or by any means, including photocopying, recording, or other electronic or mechanical methods, without the prior written permission of the author.

Book design by Queekpub

INTRODUCTION

We are truly in one of the most challenging times the world has ever seen. While many people Wake Up thinking life may be over because of all the things they see, hear or have gone through, there is a group of people that realize that tough times don't last, but tough people do. These are risk-takers. These are the people who don't stand there looking at the obstacles. Instead, they focus on what they want to do, where they want to go and what they truly want to accomplish. That's building a life by design.

Here is what we must know: the life we desire is waiting for us to rise to it. Our dreams won't come down to where we are to meet us. Our dreams depend on what we do today that others won't do, so we can have in the future what others won't have.

Knowing this, what are you going to do about it? Where will you be in five years if you continue thinking, believing and speaking as if this is it for you, and there's nothing more to live for? You must realize you don't get in life simply what you want.

You get in life what you are, and that means being willing to rise above all that's going on to be the person who attracts your dreams.

It takes more than just wishing, daydreaming or hoping for better. It takes an Unshakeable F.O.C.U.S.

CONTENT

Introduction i

Chapter 1: Find Out What You Want 1

Chapter 2: Overcome Adversity with Persistence............................. 11

Chapter 3: Concentrate on Your Dream through Imagination 23

Chapter 4: Use Your Faith 32

Chapter 5: Suggest The Positive 41

1
FIND OUT WHAT YOU WANT

We give negative energy reality by giving time and effort toward it. The only thing that should occupy our minds daily is our dreams.

- Jermain Miller

Is Your Runway Clear?

In my book *Wake Up & Win*, I recount an experience I had while sitting on an airplane, getting ready to take off. As we circled towards the runway, the plane came to an abrupt stop. After a few moments, the passengers started to get a little concerned. Nothing was said.

Finally, the pilot comes over the intercom. He said that we couldn't move at the moment, and left it at that. We all looked out our windows, but nobody seemed to see anything.

By now, we were getting extremely anxious.

As I sat, I thought about all the people going somewhere that day. Some were taking off to start their new life, a new job, vacation, conferences or school. It made me think of how everyone has somewhere to go in life. We all have a destination. We may not be going to the same places, or have the same reasons for our journeys, but we are all going somewhere.

Then, the pilot's voice comes over the intercom again. "We can't move the plane until the family of ducks clears the runway."

I thought, *We can't move this big airplane until this small family of ducks clears a runaway?*

Now, take a moment and think about being the pilot of this airplane. You have a schedule, and it's very important to focus on your destination. But right now, you have to wait for these ducks.

Many of us stay grounded for years by life's events. We call them setbacks and hardships, but in reality, they are actually very small. But because we focus so much of our attention on these obstacles, we never get to the destination of our dreams.

Here is what I learned that day. People are waiting for you to get to your destination, because by getting to your destination, you will inspire them to get to theirs. The challenges we go through in life are never really about us. They are about overcoming them to grow into the person we will become, and using that experience to impact others.

Think of how long you have wasted time, worrying about the ducks of fear. The time burdened by anxiety and guilt. Think of how you let the ducks of procrastination and over-analyzing keep this powerful human being grounded from accomplishing your dream.

Now, I want you to really think about this one: How many years have been lost simply waiting for your runway to be clear? How many lives could you have helped reach their own dreams, if only you had focused on your dream? How many times did you say to yourself, "I need to get myself together first"?

Yes, it's important to make sure your runway is clear. It's also important not to spend so much time waiting for it to clear that you never take off for your destination.

What Are You Focused On?

I found myself consumed by all that is going on in the world, and I asked myself a few big questions the other day.

"What could I do to leave a lasting impact on the lives of people? What could I accomplish in these times that people will remember me by? What is it that I really want?"

These questions immediately changed what I gave attention to. I wanted to find those answers by reaching those goals. By being remembered for doing something I really wanted to do that impacted the lives of others.

Take a moment and ask yourself the same question. What do you want? What would give your life meaning? What would wake you up every morning without an alarm clock? What would you do if you knew you could do it? Who would you be because of it? Would you be someone of value, someone of influence, someone with the purpose of being a positive force in the world?

Are you focused on your dreams, your goals and the life you wanted to see for yourself? Are you a risk-taker, someone who is willing to do the things today that others won't do so you can have the things in the future that others won't have? Or are these times causing you to become a volunteer victim who focuses on all the wrong going on in the world? Are you letting your life be dictated by circumstances, simply allowing life to happen and in the process becoming negative and depressed?

Life is always demanding more from you. The

question is, what are you willing to do about it? It's begging you to become more so that you can have more. The trouble lies in the fact that we don't know that in order to win in life and live the life of our dreams, we have to do something first before we can be.

The *doing* is in what we focus on. The *being* is the person we desire to be, regardless of our situation now. The being attracts the things we want in life. Just daydreaming or wishful thinking is not going to manifest the life we desire. We must have something to focus on, something to aim at, someone to BE.

We need a target. Many people fail in life not because they aim too high and miss. They fail because they aim too low, and that's what they hit. Too often, we have low standards, low ideas, low vision — and, most importantly — low dreams. Because of our low aim, we simply don't believe in ourselves. Unfortunately, that becomes apparent in how we think about ourselves, what we say to ourselves, and what we ultimately do or not do.

Today, even in the midst of the most challenging times, people around the world are experiencing tremendous breakthroughs. They are becoming happier, richer, healthier and living a life full of meaning. Why? Because they've decided that tough times don't last, but tough people do.

If we are going to build the life of our dreams, we have to remember that no matter what is going wrong in the world right now, we don't want to go wrong with it. We will remain focused on what we want to accomplish. The people who succeed are the people who have a definition of who they want to be. They know what they want to do and have. It is this dream that wakes them up every morning, and it's also a dream beyond the material things. These people dream of seeing the world better than what it is now, and of helping make that dream a reality. They make an effort to impact and empower people to live their dreams, because they are living examples not in words alone, but in action. These are the people that know what they want and keep going after it, despite the adversity.

Do they have adversity? Of course. No one is exempt from adversity, and it is not reserved for a special group of people. Everyone has adversity, but it's in this adversity that we are met with the only person that holds us back from achieving our dreams and goals—YOU!

Adversity is not looking for you to complain about it or cry about it or even run away from it. What it asks is, "Are you ready to have what you said you wanted? Because if you want it, you're going to have to grow through these circumstances and focus on it in order to be promoted to the next level."

Yes, even in the most trying times, people are winning. This is because adversity only reveals who we are to ourselves. It is at this point we can refer to the African Proverb: "If there is no enemy within, the enemy without can do us no harm." That means we can no longer hide or blame people or things for going wrong. We finally take a look at life and say, "This is not what I want, but now I know what I do. Now that my goals are clear, I will no longer focus on the things that are holding me hostage." It's at this point we take full responsibility, and we define what we want.

What will help you win in these times is finding out what you want and being laser-focused on believing it will happen. I call that Unshakeable FOCUS. Not only do we need to be laser-focused, but we must believe we can accomplish what we want. Our belief must be based upon conviction. We have to be inspired; otherwise, we will only be making believe we believe.

We must have a target and shut out all things that take us away from it. Having a target allows us to talk ourselves there until we get there. There is no way to hit something we are not aiming at or clear about. When we are focused, we zero in on what we want, and nothing else matters. Not a job loss, not the economy, not the failed relationships, not the health issues, the money concerns, not even the *how* of are we going to make it.

We sometimes spend so much of our energy on how we will make it when that energy should be spent thinking and working to make it. Yes, we know this is not the life we want, and we are clear on that. Still, until what we focus on changes, we will continue getting what we always got because we can't see anything different. We are blocked from accomplishing what we want because we simply don't F.O.C.U.S.

- We don't know what we want, or we don't know how to FIND it.
- We feel like we can't OVERCOME the current circumstances to get there.
- We don't CONCENTRATE long enough on our dreams.
- We are not USING our God-given talents and abilities.
- We SUGGEST too many negative things to ourselves or allow people to do the same.

For us to accomplish our dreams, one thing must happen. We must know without a shadow of a doubt what we want and focus on it. So, I want to ask you today the Big Question, and before you move forward, I want you to really think about it deeply.

What do you want?

If you're not sure, ask yourself these questions:

1. What would you want if it were impossible for you to fail?
2. What would you do if you let go of the things you hold on to from the past?
3. What would you want if you moved yourself out of the way?
4. How would you live your life if you accomplished everything you wanted to? This is one question we need to ask ourselves seriously, no matter where we are and what we may be experiencing right now.

Repeat these affirmations to clear your runway and help you focus on accomplishing your dreams.

I know the truth about me. I am powerful, healthy, successful and prosperous. I see myself doing all that I desire to do. I am focused.

The days of my yesterday life are dead and buried. I have disconnected myself from it once and for all. I live the new life of success and power of self-mastery and all accomplishment.

Within me are infinite powers seeking expression. In the past, because I did not know of their existence, they have been held back and suppressed. Now that I know this, I will focus my energy so that they shall be called into activity. Through my powers, I shall find full expression in my body in the form of perfect health, in my life in the form of success and achievement, and in my heart in the form of a mighty upwelling of joy and happiness.

2
OVERCOME ADVERSITY WITH PERSISTENCE

Our break in life comes when we have been persistent enough to break the thing that, for so long, has been breaking us.

- Jermain Miller

Consistent Persistence

For most of our lives, we have been going through circumstances we don't want because we feel like we don't have any control over what's happening to us. We persist in simply accepting the hard times, the struggle, the adversity, the pain and fear because we feel this is something we must go through. However, often what we are going through has no real purpose because we have never determined a definite place we want to end up. Where we want to go is a place undefined or simply away from whatever hardship we may be facing at the moment, and we feel this is what has to happen to get there.

Have you ever found yourself saying, "Every time I turn around, something wrong is going on" or "As soon as I start moving forward toward something good, everything seems to fall apart?" What did you do the moment after you said that? Usually, we say this right before we quit, because things just became too challenging. We have not accomplished what we think we should have. This is when we throw in the towel.

But if everyone accomplished their dreams the moment they set out to do them, would they be considered dreams? If we didn't have challenges on the way to our dreams, how would we grow in the process? If we knew how to do the things we wanted to do the moment we felt we wanted to, would they be considered goals or checklist items?

Too often, we persist in the very things we don't want because all we do is spend time thinking about them. But life was not designed for us to stand still, stay stuck and focus on the drama of life. We will never achieve our goals that way.

Goals cause us to become different types of people in order to achieve them. Something within us has to change. We must rise to the goal; the goal does not rise to us. The person that we must be has the mindset of *I will not accept life as it is now. There is something more for me. I can do more, have more and be more.* What we must realize is we can't accomplish our dreams with the same level of thinking we are used to having.

Life wants you to grow to the person you must be in order to attract the goal you said you wanted. You can't achieve your goals being the same person you were the last decade, year, month—or even the moment you decided. You must persist in becoming a new person. However, in order to persist in something, you must believe that what's possible for others is also possible for you. If you don't have faith in the life you want to live, who you want to be or what you want to do, you won't persist in getting there. You will believe it's too much of a challenge, as nice as it sounds when you talk about it.

When we do move towards our dreams, our circumstances will begin to change—everything starts to shake up. Although the shaking is good for us, things seem out of place, and we run back to put things in place instead of being focused on where we want to be. To reach our goals, we must persist until life gets better, circumstances change, or the dream appears.

Nothing happens without persistent effort toward the goal. Every day we are doing one of two things: We are either persistently going away from our dream or persistently going toward it.

Our current reality is a manifestation of what we are persistent toward.

What I See about Me Determines My Persistence
In *Wake Up & Win,* I talked about the growth of an oak tree. These powerful trees grow up to one hundred feet high, and they are massive. The oak tree has a very long life span of five hundred years, yet it produces only a single acorn during its first thirty years. Remember, the oak tree's purpose in life is to produce acorns. Acorns are the seeds of more trees.

During the next forty-four years, the oak tree produces acorns, but now it does so inconsistently. Here is where most people quit, discouraged by the inconsistent results in life. They don't hold the image of who they want to be, what they want to do and what they want to have. So the ups and downs of life cause them to say, "What's the use of all of this? It's just not worth it."

What we don't realize is that the ups and downs are only the result of us not being persistent and focused on our goals. We just don't have the faith that what we are going after will finally happen for us. During the oak tree's first seventy-four years, it had to deal with rain, hurricanes, storms, other trees dying and the risk of getting knocked down for wood. In year seventy-five, though, it does something magical. It finally grows to its maximum height and starts to produce the acorns consistently.

Just like the oak tree, we too must realize that the only way we can achieve our dreams is by being persistent. Yes, things may not look like what we wish, but we must have the end goal of growing to our maximum height by being all we can be so we can attract what we really want to attract.

Why We Must Persist

Henry David Thoreau once said, "If one advances confidently in the direction of his dreams, and endeavors to live the life which he has imagined, he will meet with a success unexpected in common hours."

In order to meet with a success unexpected in common hours, we must persist in reaching our dreams. Though we may not know when it will appear, we are confident that it will. Persistence is the main reason we win in life. We can see ourselves getting what we want despite the challenges. Usually, what holds us back is not the circumstances themselves, but the image we have of ourselves and the dream in the midst of them. We don't persist because we are not confidently advancing in the direction of our dreams. Instead, we fear. We don't see ourselves winning. Yes, circumstances are real, but we have the power within to overcome them if we persist and have the right image of ourselves in the process.

This means moving beyond the point where we thought we were going to quit. It means remembering what we felt when we gave up last time. It's a reminder of when we heard the word no and decided not to go back. It's no longer being afraid of putting all our faith in the attainment of our dream. We know that what we set out to accomplish is not an easy journey. There is a fight all the way, but we must realize that it's a fight we can win.

Sometimes it may seem like life is bullying us, as if an invisible force has been set up to challenge us and hold us back. Here is a secret, though: this is when life tests how much we believe in our ideas and goals. Is this something we really wanted, or was it something we were just wishing for or aimlessly speaking about? When the bullies of life realize we mean business and will persist, these bullies seem to disappear, and the journey becomes easier.

We won't achieve the success we are looking for in life if we are not persistent. If you have had trouble persisting, here are a few things that may be holding you back:

Weak dreams or goals
When we have weak dreams or goals, they bring weak results. Weak desires do not go to the core of us. Instead, they are just distractions that we easily give up and move on to the next, never achieving our true goals. Whatever you want to accomplish must be definite. Know what you want and develop an interest in it.

Procrastination
Too often, we are waiting for the right moment to jump in, when the coast is clear and there is no traffic on the road. This is indecision. Indecision is a decision, but it's a decision to fail—because we procrastinate. Often we use elaborate excuses as to why we simply won't start. We must remember the time will never be perfect—there will always be a challenge to overcome. But mostly, the challenge is having faith that we can do what we desire to do.

Unclear goals

Successful people are clear about what they want. They are always working toward their goals, seeing, believing and being before doing what they need to do to reach their dreams. They visualize. In contrast, unsuccessful people are always having things done to them. They are not sure what they want. They only visualize all the wrong that could happen and never get any closer to their success.

Compromising

Sometimes we settle for less because we don't want to work as hard. We compromise with ourselves and say we'll start working towards our goals later, when we have more time or money. But we never get what we want, because we keep settling for something less.

Looking for a shortcut

The way to success is rarely an easy route. Looking for shortcuts or bargaining the cost will not help us reach our dreams and goals. Instead, we become more focused on avoiding obstacles than overcoming them. We must be ready and willing to do the work required to accomplish our goal.

Our break in life comes when we have been persistent enough to break the thing that, for so long, has been breaking us.

How to Stay Persistent

Whenever we are going through circumstances in life, we identify with them. How we view ourselves determines whether we overcome adversity or succumb to it. The good news is, if adversity has been a constant bully in our lives and life has been whipping us to the point of exhaustion, we can change that any moment by identifying with a new image.

Beginning to see these setbacks as opportunities is the key to identifying with a new image. When we trust the struggle is worth it, we overcome fear. We face these obstacles despite fear. We decide that we will no longer be pushed around, because the person we are becoming is not the person who gives up. It does not matter what we have gone through in life or how things may seem at this moment. What matters is what we see for ourselves going forward. We do not have to stay connected to what has happened in the past. We don't have to let the same mistakes keep replaying in our lives. We can change our self-image by believing better things can happen now, not simply waiting for things to get better in some unknown future.

We must identify with an image that will inspire us

to make the right decisions, take immediate action and fight toward the future that we desire.

Those images can be the following:

Affirmations: *Something powerful that we agree with. Something we can commit to saying every day despite the appearance of things. We must see ourselves as healthy, whole, successful and happy. We must know that every day, in every way, we are getting better and better.*

Pictures: *I once heard a picture is worth a thousand words. What pictures are you surrounded by that keep you motivated, striving, and inspired to be, do and have?*

Family: *This can be the biggest motivating factor and inspiration. When your self-image changes for the better, so will the lifestyle of your family.*

These images of a better life will help you start to believe that better is possible for you. You will believe you are entitled to the life of your dreams.

One of the reasons change is difficult is because too often, all of our efforts at change were directed at the images outside us. We wanted our circumstances to change first, without truly understanding why they were the way they were. To really live the life of our dreams, we must have an image of who we want to be. We must always be striving toward that image. We have to believe in ourselves when other people don't. We have to motivate ourselves and see ourselves in possession of the life we want to live.

As challenging as that may seem, WE have to look in the mirror and say, "Yes, I can have a new self-image and know what the truth is." We must refuse to remain locked in some false image of our past. Someone's negative opinion does not have to be your reality, and that includes your own!

By removing our self-imposed limitations, we can begin to enlarge our self-image. In my book *Wake Up & Win*, I compare positive self-image growth to a seed. When a farmer plants his seeds in the ground, he has an image of his harvest, so he works to make it true. He trusts in the process, even if he can't see the change yet. He cultivates the land until it manifests its harvest.

Like the farmer, we must do the same thing in our lives. We have to plant the seed of a positive self-image and tend to our garden until it manifests. Persistence requires faith. In order to stay persistent, we must have a strong purpose and a desire to bring that purpose to life. Persistence turns desire into reality, and as our plans become real, we will gain confidence in our dreams.

When you persist in something, you are winning it already. Every day you work towards your dreams brings them closer to reality. Stay on the right path and take small steps towards your goals. See each day as a victory, and start living the life of your dreams!

Below are daily affirmations to help you stay persistent on the path to your dreams.

I have decided who I want to be, what I want to do and have, and I now see it in my mind.

I have the ability to accomplish my dream. Every day I see myself in possession of it. I am using my visualization to see only the good in my life. Because I see the good, I persist in it.

3
CONCENTRATE ON YOUR DREAM THROUGH IMAGINATION

If you look at your dreams as they are, they become worse than they are. But if you imagine your dreams as they could be, they become what they should be.

- Jermain Miller

Imagination Alteration

We all have an image of what we want our world to look like now and in the future. Our imagination is always working. We have imagined who we are and what we have now, consciously or unconsciously. If we do not imagine the life we want to live, the person we want to be and the dreams we want to accomplish, we are still imagining — but we are not imagining what we really want. We are, by default, imagining a life we don't want to live.

Love, health, wealth and success are what we dream of, but those dreams can seem elusive when we think of ourselves actually having them. For many of us, all that we know comes from our past experiences. Our memory contains all the facts we use to determine whether or not we believe we can actually accomplish our dreams. Too often, these facts are typically the mistakes we made: a failed business or bad marriage, or ideas, goals and dreams we decided not to act upon. Who we believe we are is based on our past experiences, and we relive it over and over as if there were no way out. But by doing so, we operate out of our memory and not out of our imagination.

How often do you let yourself be upset about the mistakes of the past—the fears or the failed attempts at what you could have done or should have done? We store the images of each incident and feeling of failure, and that paralyzes us. In many cases, it seems as though because of our past, our future must mirror that. It's true that we can't just leave behind the mistakes of the past; those hardships and setbacks really did happen, and they helped shape us into who we are today. But we can break free of that troubled past by searching our memory, as painful as it can be, and realizing why we made the mistakes we did.

If we are going to change our future, we must change our now. We have to imagine ourselves being the person we want to be, doing the things we desire and having everything we've dreamed of. This is one of the most important discoveries we can make. We can't attempt to change our circumstances from negative to positive before we change the image we have of them. We may not be able to stop what comes in our minds, but we can stop how we think, feel and what we do when the negative thoughts come. Knowing this will help us stop wearing ourselves out fighting negative ideas. We must realize that our own minds are operating with these negative powers, and it is this we need to alter.

Concentrate on Your Dream through Imagination
Years ago, homeless and having lost just about everything at twenty-five years old, I woke up sleeping on a basement floor, staring at the ceiling. I had pennies in my pocket and ninety-three cents in my bank account. I had, in my opinion, hit rock bottom.

Clearly, I was living a nightmare, and I needed some kind of inspiration if I were to turn things around.

I started reading a book entitled *Live Your Dreams* by Les Brown, and a line in his book changed my life forever. "You have something special; you have greatness in you."

I had never heard such a powerful line before. I began looking at my current place in life and asked myself the question that would turn things around: Jermain, in five years, if you keep doing what you are doing now, where would you be?

I knew deep down I could not endure how things were for me at the moment, and I believe that's where most people are. They know they can't continue to endure what they are going through, but they simply can't imagine what they want for their lives. In order for me to overcome where I was, I had to replace how I saw myself with what I saw I could be. I believed it was possible to be rich, happy and successful. To be loved and be mentally, physically and spiritually well. I truly believed it; I just didn't believe it was possible for me.

At that point, I had no choice but to give myself two options. Either I Wake Up and Live the greatest life of my dreams, or I continue to drag through life with no purpose or meaning. I chose to Live. Years later, I found myself at an event for the first time with Les Brown live. I thought to myself as I sat in the audience, I'd give anything to be in his life, and I'm going to tell him that when I finally get to take a picture with him. Little did I know the ticket I purchased was the wrong one, and I was not able to take the picture with him and tell him how my life turned around because of it. I was devastated and went back to my seat in agony. Instead of moping around, though, I decided I would not be in his life as a picture-taker, but as his spiritual son.

Considering I was in an audience of 5000 people, anyone I told this to would have thought I was insane. But I didn't focus on the steps. I didn't focus on how long it would take. Too often, when we decide to reach for our dreams, we get overwhelmed by trying to picture the individual steps it will take to get there.

Instead, I imagined myself day in and day out speaking to him on the phone, speaking at events with him and, most importantly, encouraging the encourager. Less than two years later, I found myself at the same event in another city. This time, I was backstage with Les Brown, supporting him as he motivated a crowd of thousands. I remembered sitting in the audience, saying to myself, "One day." Now, that day was finally here.

While being backstage watching one of the most powerful speakers of our time was incredible, what was even more amazing was the relationship that we developed before I even got there. It was everything I had imagined in detail. This is what I had seen in

my mind, and regardless of what happened along the way, I never stopped imagining what I wanted to happen.

How to Manifest What You Imagine

If we continue to imagine the drama, the hard times, the pain or the guilt and shame, we will not manifest anything else. What we persist in imagining eventually becomes our reality. The difficulty lies in imagining what we want, regardless of what we may be experiencing at the moment, and holding that image steady until what we really want appears. Everything you want to be, do and have is already created and waiting for you. It is not on the way; it already is. The gap is between where you are now in your imagination and where you want to be in the future. You never have to search for what you are. You simply must become the person that attracts the things you want in your imagination.

Keep the pictures of what you want in front of you. This is the key to manifestation. You must have the picture of what you want in front of you at all times. It does not matter if it's a spouse, an income you desire, the business of your dreams, happiness or overcoming the challenges of life. Having the right image will motivate you to get to it. Visualize it daily as best as you can. See every detail of the picture; see it as a reality. This will require you to work at it—you have to train yourself to imagine the good. Then, get up and do what you can to help bring what you picture to pass. Remember, what you are dominated by mentally will one day take shape physically.

The more powerful the imagination, the more powerful the attraction.

We are magnets. We can attract negative just as much as we attract positive. Doubt and fear will destroy what we imagine and demagnetize our attraction. In order to attract the positive, we must:

Believe in it
Dream it
Eat with it
Sleep with it

This is how we become one with it. This is what is called burning desire—when we become so in tune with what we want that it's only a matter of time before it happens. We become so immersed in what we imagine that nothing stands in the way of us getting it. We become so confident in the feeling of what we imagine that we are it until it appears.

Abandon all limited thinking.
Limited thinking translates to:

I don't see myself doing that.
I don't think this is possible for me.
Everyone else seems to have it, but I doubt I can.

This is what I refer to in Chapter 1 as Clearing Your Runway. If you are going to achieve the highest heights of your imagination, you have to clear your limited thinking. This is something you must work on repeatedly, day in and day out.

Let go of resentment.
Usually the reason we can't imagine ourselves at our best is because we don't let go of resentment. We still hold on to fear, guilt and hate towards others but, more importantly, ourselves. Living this way shuts down the flow in our lives. If we want to flow freely and see clearly, we will need to let go of the negative feelings that hold us back, even if we feel we are right to hold on to them.

You may be feeling like life may be over, or things

are too overwhelming for you to move forward. The truth is, where you are now is not your final destination in life. Your circumstances are not your conclusion. You may feel as if there is some force stopping you from getting to your dreams, but the truth is, concentrating on your dream through imagination will help you to realize it.

Our imagination is the bridge to our future. In order for our future to become our present, we have to think of the end dream, not where we are now. If you want to break free of where you are in life and transform your world, you need to imagine that you are already what you want to be. You have to feel the way you would expect to feel under the circumstances. If you change your imagining, you will change your facts.

Say these affirmations daily to strengthen your imagination and build your bridge to your new future.

I now imagine my world as I wish to live in it. I live there in mind now. Knowing this, I transport myself from where I am currently to where I want to be in my future.

My imagination creates my reality. Now that I am aware of what I imagine, I am aware of what I am creating.

My future is not in the hands of anyone else. My future is in my hands, because I am imagining it.

4
USE YOUR FAITH

It's not what we have faith IN that ultimately determines our manifestation; it's our faith.

- Jermain Miller

I hope, I believe, I know

Have you ever stopped for a moment and asked yourself, "Why can't I get what I want out of life?"

The truth is, if we are not mentally ready to receive the things we say we want, we will never receive them. To achieve our dreams, we must be ready. We must have faith.

We never stand still in our faith. Either we are growing in faith, accomplishing our dreams in the process, or we are going backwards, not believing anything is possible for us.

We can only attract to ourselves what we have an image of. Therefore, it follows that if we want to attract larger things, we must have larger images. Often, when we find ourselves falling short in what we believe can happen for us, we stop. We lose faith, and we can't seem to see beyond a certain point. We stop growing.

There are many reasons why we stop thinking larger for ourselves. One of them is the loss of faith in achieving better than where we are. We convince ourselves that our lives cannot be better than they are. We may talk as though life could be better. We may even feel as though we deserve a better life. But in most cases, secretly, we don't believe we do. We speak highly of our goals and dreams in the moment, but we don't have faith that what we want will happen.

We operate under the idea that "This is as far as I can see myself going. I can't imagine anything more to come. I can only believe in what has already happened." That idea causes us to beat ourselves down and become fearful. In that fear, we unconsciously do something that destroys our chances of actually getting the things we want from life. This self-sabotage is dangerous, and it causes us to lose faith in us. But since it comes from within, it is something in our power to change.

We must know that there are no limitations to what we can do. It is not life that limits us, but our faith in what we can produce. Our only limitation is our lack of belief that life can give us more than what we have right now. We are not limited by boundaries, walls, roadblocks or obstacles, but by false ideas about who we are and what we can accomplish. We fail to recognize what we are truly dealing with. We must become what we want to manifest, but we will never be able to do that while we still persist in seeing what we do not want. We cannot have true faith in something if we doubt the possibility of it happening. We will never manifest the dream.

Instead of dwelling on our failures and difficulties, we must have the faith that what we truly want will happen once we start working towards it. One of the most important things to remember is that we cannot manifest a life beyond our mental ability to do so. This means that we give birth to an idea only from within ourselves. Where we choose to focus our thoughts determines whether we have the faith that what we are thinking about will materialize.

Stoplight Faith

While setting my goal to run one day, I decided that I wanted to run to a certain point in the city. The great thing about running in the city is all of the different landmarks you can see along the way to your goal. When I was about two miles from my destination, I was exhausted. I knew that if I did those full two miles,

I'd also have to run back an extra two miles to get back home. As I ran, I thought, "I can just come back tomorrow and do this. Or maybe I should just forget this and run a different route."

However, this is not what I set out to do. I wanted to get to my destination. As I looked up, I realized something. While the blocks were long, there were only six stoplights between me and my destination. I thought to myself, "I will get to the first light and assess how I feel once I get there." When I accomplished the goal of getting to the first light, I realized that there was enough energy in me to get to the next light—and so on until I finally made it to my destination. I built up my faith in myself by not quitting when I didn't feel like going on. Instead, I gave myself smaller things to have faith in. I decided to just make it to the next stoplight, and then the next one. And that ultimately helped me get to my bigger goal.

One of the reasons we don't accomplish what we set out to is because our goals and dreams may seem too large to achieve. While it is important to have big goals, we must set obtainable goals that we can reach along the way. We cannot look to hit the home run without trying to get on base first. In order for us to build our faith to get the big things we desire in life, we must learn how to have the faith in ourselves to accomplish the small things first and assess ourselves along the way. Too often, we live by the term 'Go big or go home,' and because we don't go big, we wind up staying home.

The Faith Process

In speaking to a client recently, they said to me, "Do you think I decided to be going through what I'm going through now? I'm no fool. I did not choose this."

I said, "No, you are not a fool, but it is quite possible that you have been fooled, and most of us have been." I know of no one who has escaped being fooled about life. Examine your thinking and see how many times a day you think of something that you do not want to happen. When you do that, you are focusing on the wrong thing—what you do not want instead of what you do. You are feeding the dark wolf.

Instead of thinking of what you cannot do, think of what you can. Many of us do not write our goals down because we don't have the faith that they will happen. This is self-imposed limitation. We don't actually believe deep down what we want will happen, so what sense does it make to write down what we want? Though your goal may look far away, in order for you to manifest it, you have to develop the faith you can. You must spend time with it. What are the closer goals you will meet each day as you pursue your ultimate destination? Every day, you must check in on your dream, check in on the goal, and check in on the idea. In the process, you build your faith as you start to believe that it can happen.

When we decided to go after our dream, there was no map of the journey — we only had the image of the dream. But when we started going after the dream, and things started looking too hard, too often, we got discouraged and said, "I never imagined my life would look like that." Here's what we must understand: In our mind, we only saw the dream. If we had been able to see the map of the journey and all the wrong things that were going to happen — the sacrifice, the worry, the setbacks, the hardships and the loss — we would probably say, "No way I'm paying that price for my dream."

Instead of wanting a map to your dream, you must know what you want and identify what your dream is. In the process of reaching your dream, you will struggle through some times when things seem to be going the opposite of what you want in your life, like having money, health, family or relationship issues.

You must remember that although these challenges are not part of your dream, they are an important part of the process. They are part of the process to build your faith.

Our goals are like a seed, and seeds take time to grow. If we plant a seed in the ground, then dig up the seed after a week if we have not seen any growth, we will never have a crop to reap. Instead, we should tend to the seed, and make sure it has enough water and sun. We can give it some fertilizer and keep the weeds from growing around it. But we must leave the seed in the ground. If we take the seed out of the ground and try to plant it somewhere else, and then somewhere else, we are interrupting its process, and it will never grow. Instead of digging up our goals and looking for new ground, we need to tend to the ground we have. We must not interrupt our faith process.

Great Faith Brings Great Things

Life is limitless. The only thing that's limited is what we have faith in. Whatever we believe in, our faith in it must be large enough to support what we desire. A small thought will produce only a small thing.

Many people stop believing in their dreams because they have never really accomplished something big in their lives. They do not believe in their possibilities, but in their limitations. Yes, we must look at our challenges, but only so we can overcome them. Never see only your limitations. Never dwell on them, and, most importantly, do not talk about your limitations to anyone. This is the only way to grow in faith. A person with great faith is the person who does great things in life. Get a hold of the biggest thing you can think of and claim it for your own; see yourself in possession of it, and you will prove to yourself that life is without bounds. You can come back from wherever you are if you have the faith you can.

Faith is about seeing and believing even when what you want is not in appearance. By repeating these affirmations below every day, you will grow your faith and destroy your doubt.

I am that larger thing. I am now entering into that larger life. I feel that something within is drawing more to me. Every day, I live with the idea and let that concept grow. I am only expecting the biggest and the best to happen to me.

I no longer let small thoughts come into my mind. I have the faith that I will experience larger and greater victories in my life. I will not let go of what I see for myself until I manifest it.

I destroy all negative thoughts I wish not to experience and replace them with what I wish to.

I have faith in myself that I have the power to do big things. I realize that if my faith is small, I will only do small things. Since my faith is big, the things I attract to my life are big also.

5
SUGGEST THE POSITIVE

*We were not given the vision for the journey.
We were given the vision for the dream.*

- Jermain Miller

Repetition Keeps Us There

The appearance of things in life depends not on what we see, but on what we tell ourselves when we look at it. We tell ourselves we've been working for years, but life keeps on wearing us down. Roll with the punches is the term we use, but we keep getting beaten up. Still, we say, that's life.

But have you noticed how it's different for some people? They keep going, through the hard times and on to the good. That's because life has a way of appearing to be one way for one person and another way for the other. The difference between the person who makes it and the one who doesn't is what they repeatedly say to themselves in these times.

Robert Schiller once said, "Tough times don't last, but tough people do." Challenging times will cease to seem so difficult when we change our conversations with ourselves in the midst of them.

I was sitting at a railroad crossing in my car recently. As I sat and waited for the train to come by, I put my car in park and let it idle until the train passed. When it was safe to continue on my journey, I thought about those moments in life where we may have so many things coming at us so fast that we never take a moment to make sure we are clear before moving forward. We find ourselves going in reverse, where we have the fears of yesterday, or jumping ahead even though the path is not clear. Instead of jumping backward into doubt or ahead into danger, we have to be able to stop and idle our engines until we can clearly see the road ahead. We must know where we are going and why we want to get there.

We do not get to where we want simply by wishing—we get there by what we say. Our power lies in what we suggest to ourselves when a decision must be made. Do I continue moving forward in chaos, do I continue going backward into doubt and fear—or do I take a deep breath, think about where I want to be and suggest all the reasons why I should be there?

Suggestion is one of the most powerful forces in the world. It has equal power in two directions: positive and negative, depending on where you focus your energy.

Suggestion can be used to discipline and control ourselves, and in its most magnificent way, it can construct the most beautiful life we can imagine. Most of the time, if we are honest with ourselves, we spend more time suggesting the negative than the positive. Have you ever noticed the more you speak about something, the more likely it is to manifest? Yes, this also happens when we speak negatively as well. Why is that? Well, it's simple — where our intensity goes, our energy flows. The intensity of our conversations with ourselves determines the intensity of what appears in our lives.

Where we are today is based on what we repeatedly said to ourselves in the past. Where we will be in the future is based on what we repeatedly say to ourselves today. We have shaped our current lives and will shape our future through our words.

Have you ever found yourself repeating the following:
I'm not attractive

I just can't
I'm a failure/I will fail
I don't have a chance
I don't deserve this
I'm too young/old to start working on my dreams
Other people can do that, but that's not for me
I messed up so much in the past
I'm not good enough
I'm broke
I've lost so many years doing this, I can't possibly come back from it

Are these negative suggestions true about you? Of course not, but here is what happens — we persist in these conversations based on what we see or feel until they become a reality. And then, we continue to talk about the reality we have created.

Neville Goddard once said, "An assumption, though false, if persisted in, will harden into fact." If we make assumptions based on negative suggestions, those assumptions become our reality because we persist in them, even though they are negative. When the world does not appear to be as you think it should, what kind of conversations do you have? What are you constantly telling yourself you cannot do, have or be? I don't mean the conversations we have with friends or family, when we vent or commiserate. The conversations I'm referring to are the secret conversations we have with ourselves.

What do we tell ourselves when we are all alone? When we don't think we will be able to overcome the challenges we're going through? We may say to ourselves in the mirror, "I want to be successful, happy or in love." But then we negate it by saying, "Honestly, I can't see myself having that or doing it." These words make us unhappy about who we are and what we can accomplish, yet at the same time, we get comfortable with them and talk ourselves right out of our goals and dreams.

These secret conversations with ourselves determine where we end up. Our inner conversations can push us toward success, or they can keep us in a corner in fear.

They can push us to greatness or talk us into a mediocre life unfulfilled. They can hinder our growth and keep us stagnant when we want to walk away from what we know stopped our progress. We allow ourselves to be controlled by our negative words because we don't believe what we say matters to our future. So, in essence, we talk ourselves right out of the life we desire.

Think of a team building a house. If there are defects in the plans and they don't know about them, those defects will appear in the completed building. Life is similar. In these suggestions we make to ourselves, we are either strengthening or undermining our process. If we accept what we tell ourselves, our mind is acting upon it — for good or bad.

Conversation Switch

Within us all is the possibility of success. To start, we need to turn those negative self-talks into positive ones. It is just as easy to see ourselves as a success as it is a failure.

Today, start a new practice. Begin by releasing past mistakes, the things you thought you should have done, the people you thought you should have been with and where you feel you should have been by now. The fact is, you are where you are at this moment, and at this moment, you are aware of where you want to be.

Now that you are here, what you say to and about yourself needs to change. You begin by holding the self-image of the person you want to be in your mind. Know who you want to be, do and have, and talk to yourself as if you were that person. See yourself having all the things you want to have, doing all the things you want to do and being all that you want to be. This is the person we all can become.

Be aware of how you speak of yourself and your circumstances. Be careful with your words. If something negative is about to come out of your mouth, be disciplined enough to realize those words won't bring positive results. Ask yourself, would the successful me say this about me or what's going on in my life now?

We must realize that we can't continue holding low opinions of ourselves. If we want to advance toward our goals and dreams, we have to stop carrying around a mental picture of a victim. Instead, we must concentrate on constructive ideas, high goals, greater success, and new images about who we can become. It's time to let go of the toxic, unnecessary, self-imposed limits that have restricted our full realization of potential through what we say. We are all the product of our thoughts and experiences up to this point. Where we choose to direct our own course going forward through life is totally up to us.

When our image of ourselves changes, so does what we believe. And, what we believe changes what we say, which ultimately changes the world around us. We must take ownership of what we say about ourselves and our ability to accomplish our dreams and goals. We no longer can speak low of ourselves and expect greatness to appear. Instead, we must learn how to elevate ourselves and our world by elevating our conversations. We can immediately start to do this in a few easy ways:

Stop spending time asking questions on how you will overcome adversity.

If we continue talking about adversity, what else do we think will appear? We cannot speak of what we don't want while not speaking of what we do want. In doing this, we hold adversity in our lives and give it more power than it should have.

Stop speaking of yourself or the things we may be going through in a discouraging way.

When we do this, we are planting the seeds that stop forward progress. We plant fear, worry and procrastination. We must find positive, constructive ways to encourage ourselves, even when the way forward is challenging and unclear.

Don't speak of failure in a way that causes you to focus on failure as a possibility.

Yes, life may seem tough, but why continue to give our energy to the tough circumstances? This same energy could be used to speak ourselves into the person we want to be. Remember, action follows any conversation we have with ourselves, and action is nothing more than energized thought.

Ask yourself, "What are the people around me saying to me?"

Believe it or not, people make suggestions to us all day, every day. We must ask ourselves, "Who are these people around me? What do they have me doing, thinking and, most importantly, saying?" Sometimes, the closest people to us mean well in what they say to us, even when it is negative. But because they are close to us, we don't want to hurt them by spending less time with them or telling them they are negative.

In *Wake Up & Win*, I discuss Abraham Maslow's great words of advice: "We are doing one of two things — we are stepping forward into greatness or stepping back into safety." Too often, we are stepping back into safety. We just can't see ourselves accomplishing our dreams in life, and we have lived safely. Living that way causes us to step back in fear. Our thoughts become our self-image and our habits. Our thoughts and habits determine who we believe ourselves to be, so we will not change until we change our current self-image. If we believe we can have more in life, do more and be more, we can. But to start, we have to change our self-image.

Talk Your Way through It

No matter where you are today, I want you to stop for a moment, lift your head, stick out your chest and repeat after me: "Good things are supposed to happen to me." Yes, that's right. Good things are supposed to happen to you. You may have gone through some trying times and circumstances, but those things were not supposed to break you and have you quit on life. Trials come in our lives, until they cease to be trials through growth. The more you grow from your circumstances, the less these trials have any effect on you.

When you find yourself talking negatively about yourself and your future, remind yourself that you can make it, despite everything going on. You have powers that you haven't even tapped into yet.

No one is going to believe in you until you believe in your dream. No one is going to speak highly of your goals until you do. Start seeing yourself as stronger, wiser and better. Only you can develop the Unshakeable F.O.C.U.S. required to live the life of your dreams.

Your words have power. When you find yourself speaking negatively about life and giving power to that, the affirmations below will enable you to overcome those negative conversations and remind you of who you truly are and what you truly can accomplish.

Today I am no longer speaking based on what I see. I am speaking based on what I want to see!

Each day I am improving my thoughts and what I say about me. No longer will I allow negative thoughts to take over a mind I have full control over.

Today is the day that I will overcome more of my fears, worries and other destructive thoughts and habits. They simply have no power over me.

Every day I am developing greater health, happiness and prosperity to create a better tomorrow.

My words have power. I am watching how I speak about myself. I will no longer speak in terms of I can't and I will fail. Instead, I will speak of what I can do and what I will do, which will ultimately lead me to it.

Today I choose to only speak of myself in terms of Life! Love! Health and Happiness!

Wake Up & Live:
Powerful Methods for
Achieving Your Dreams,
Overcoming Adversity
and Finding Happiness:

Wake Up & Win:
How To Reach Your
Goals And Live The Life
Of Your Dreams.